CHRISTMAS CROSS STITCH

Jutta Lammèr

 Sterling Publishing Co., Inc.   New York

Translated by Elizabeth Reinersmann
Photography by Fotostudio Thomas Weiß
Drawings by Gisele Thommel

Library of Congress Cataloging-in-Publication Data

Lammèr, Jutta.
  [Weihnachtsstickereien. English]
  Christmas cross stitch/Jutta Lammèr ; [translated by Elizabeth
Reinersmann ; drawings by Gisele Thommel].
    p. cm.
  Translation of: Weihnachtsstickereien.
  Includes index.
  ISBN 0-8069-6861-3. ISBN 0-8069-6862-1 (pbk.)
  1. Cross-stitch—Patterns. 2. Christmas decorations. I. Title.
TT778.C76L3613 1988
746.3'041—dc19

                                     88-3781
                                     CIP

3 5 7 9 10 8 6 4 2

English translation copyright 1988 by
Sterling Publishing Co., Inc.
387 Park Avenue South, New York, N.Y. 10016
Original edition published in West Germany
under the title, "Weihnachtsstickereien" © 1987
Otto Maier GmbH Ravensburg
Distributed in Canada by Sterling Publishing
℅ Canadian Manda Group, P.O. Box 920, Station U
Toronto, Ontario, Canada M8Z 5P9
Distributed in Great Britain and Europe by Cassell PLC
Artillery House, Artillery Row, London SW1P IRT, England
Distributed in Australia by Capricorn Ltd.
P.O. Box 665, Lane Cove, NSW 2066
Printed and bound in Hong Kong
All rights reserved

Sterling ISBN 0-8069-6862-1 (pbk.)

Overview

Cross-stitch—once used primarily by young girls for practicing purposes—has become popular among embroidery enthusiasts. Their ranks are growing, and a large number of men are joining in the activity.

Scandinavian countries have been particularly influential in this development with a great deal of interest being generated in Denmark through the world-renowned needlework guild "Haandarbejdets Femme" in Copenhagen under the patronage of the Danish queen. They are able to attract famous artists who create new designs, while observing the age-old traditions. Most notable among them is Gerda Bengston, who has a special gift for transposing into cross-stitch pattern the most minute details of the environment. She displayed this remarkable talent in her 1985 *Calendar of Roses*.

A less naturalistic interpretation can be found in the work of Edith Hansden and Ida Winkler. They have created beautiful motifs for the Christmas season. By making the patterns less ornamental, they convey a sense of this very special season without being too obvious. This book follows their example. The patterns are for the most part less soft, in form as in the choice of colors.

It is, of course, up to you to use the color choices in this book or, if you wish, to follow your own imagination. If you associate Christmas with the clear, crisp, and cold days of winter your choice of color and form might be more severe and austere. If, on the other hand, Christmas conjures up thoughts of coziness and warmth, of candles and baked apples you might want to choose forms and colors that match those feelings.

But, whatever you decide, it is important to schedule your project to avoid last-minute problems. For instance, the samples on page 29 (motifs suitable for Christmas cards) are relatively easy to complete, but more time is needed for other patterns, which often require several evenings or weekends of work. This is especially true for those patterns involving frequent color changes and those with larger surfaces to cover.

So—get ready to start now!

MATERIAL

Each sampler in this book (displayed on the right-hand pages) is accompanied by a pattern complete with symbols representing the corresponding color number (displayed on the left-hand pages). Each symbol represents one cross-stitch.

With the exception of the Christmas tree on pages 14–15 everything is stitched on #10.5 linen. This means: Each cm square contains 10.5 threads, counting vertically and horizontally. This will enable you to make 5.25 (5¼) cross-stitches. As an example: If an illustration consists of 110.25 by 110.25 cross-stitches the area covered will be 8.25″ × 8.25″ (21 × 21 cm). Be aware, however, that not all linen fabrics have the same thread count; they may differ by several millimeters. For instance the material used for

the Christmas tree on page 15 was not intended for embroidery. This material accommodates only 4.5 cross-stitches per cm.

Another material that is specifically designed for cross-stitching is aida cloth. Here, groups of threads are woven into equal-size squares. The two Christmas trees shown here show the difference. The dimensions of the tree on the left, stitched on linen, are 2″ × 3¼″ (5.2 × 8.2 cm). The dimensions of the tree on the right, stitched on aida cloth, are 1¾″ × 3″ (4.5 × 7.4 cm).

We used embroidery needle No. 22 and double-strand floss for all samplers in the book. Each embroidery floss has six threads to a strand and sometimes they get tangled up when being divided. By twisting the strand in the opposite direction you can easily undo the tangle.

TECHNIQUE

Cross-stitching is done in two separate steps. First you do the so-called "understitch," which is the first half of the cross-stitch that runs from the lower left to the upper right. The second step completes the cross by going from the upper right to the lower left in the opposite direction.

The variations within this technique are many. The difference shows up on the reverse side of your embroidery. The stitches might, for instance, appear as vertical or horizontal stitches or as blocks. The easiest method is the one that creates the vertical stitch on the back. The diagram on top of page 5 illustrates this method: Pull the floss through from the back to the front between two threads of the canvas. Guide the floss diagonally across one block (two threads, if linen is used) and pull it through to the back, again between threads. If you want to shorten the process you can do so at this point. Instead of pulling the floss through to the back of the canvas, guide the tip of the needle downwards across one block and pull the needle through the canvas to the front. This will create the vertical stitch in the back and at the same time be the beginning (understitch) of the next cross-stitch.

Finish each row as required, by stitching the understitch first and complete the cross-stitch by stitching the top stitch, in the opposite direction. When you do the first stitch make sure that you are able to secure the end of the floss properly. This can be best accomplished by making a slipknot from some excess floss. This later allows you to pull that excess under the backstitches.

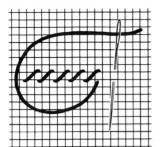 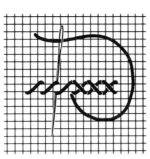

An experienced embroiderer will lay some excess floss (in the back) along the row to be stitched and cover it in the process of stitching. Whichever method you choose, never make a knot that has to remain permanently on the back of the canvas.

An equally easy technique is the one where the backstitch will be a horizontal stitch. (See diagram below.) Here you work up and down: The understitch is done by going upwards and the top stitch by coming down. For the understitch you pull the floss from the back to the front and diagonally across one block to its upper right corner. Guide the tip of the needle through to the back, then horizontally from left to right across one block and through to the front. You now have a horizontal stitch in the back and the beginning of the understitch for the next cross-stitch.

At first glance there seems little difference between these two techniques. But in closer examination it becomes clear that the cross-stitch with the vertical backstitch (working from left to

becomes more evident when a larger area has to be covered and one has a heavy hand (meaning a rather tight pull of the floss).

Choose one of the two techniques before you begin your project and stick with it. Changing between the two will result in an uneven finished product. This is true even when an embroidery frame is used. The unevenness will be obvious as soon as the canvas is removed from the frame.

A few points are worth remembering:

1. Always pull the floss *between* two canvas threads, never *through* the thread of the canvas.
2. Don't stitch through the floss of the stitches that are already in place.
3. Pull the floss evenly so that the cross-stitches have an even appearance and the canvas underneath is not bunched up.
4. Always complete both steps of a cross-stitch before changing to another color.

Working with counting instructions:

1. Determine the most central point of both your pattern and your canvas by drawing a horizontal and vertical line through the middle and marking the spot.

It is here that you begin your first stitch.

(Two threads = one block = one cross-stitch, if linen is used.)

2. Often the center of a design contains a variety of colors. This implies that many

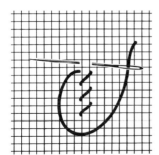 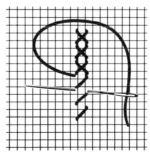

right) is somewhat taller and narrower in comparison to the one with the horizontal backstitch (working up and down). This difference

changes are necessary, which will tend to interrupt the stitching rhythm. If that is the case it makes more sense to begin your work at the center of the bottom row, working first to the left and then to the right. The sampler on pages 59–61, for instance, has many words and is a good case in point.

3. If the design is relatively small it is best to begin stitching from the lower left-hand corner and to choose the up-and-down technique with the backstitch running horizontally.

4. Avoid the temptation of starting your stitching with the border. Only *one* mistake when counting the thread will cause the whole design to be off-center and therefore off-balance. The simpler the design the easier it is to miscount.

5. The transfer of a design from the pattern to the canvas is relatively easy when the design is small. Just cut a strip from a piece of cardboard and use it as a guide, moving it from row to row according to the technique you have chosen.

6. With a more intricate design the following tip might be helpful:
    a. Make a photocopy of the pattern. Pin this copy on a thin board of Styrofoam (or a similar porous material that will hold pins in place).

    b. With two pins—one at the beginning and one at the end of the row—you are able to keep track of where your place on the pattern is.
See photo below.

FINISHING

If you have used an embroidery frame it is sufficient to remove the frame and turn your work right side down on a soft white pad and steam-iron the canvas. (If you don't have a steam iron use a damp cloth.)

If the canvas is creased from too much folding or has an indentation from the embroidery frame or is pulled out of shape, soak your finished product briefly in warm water, let it air dry on a flat surface and, while it is still damp, iron the canvas with the right side down.

If you plan on framing your embroidery, take a piece of rigid cardboard the size of the inner indentation on the back of the picture frame and fold the edges of the canvas around it. Secure the canvas to the cardboard by using long stitches, first connecting the two edges of the canvas with the longer distance between them, next connecting the edges with the shorter distance between them. Make sure the canvas is evenly pulled across the cardboard.

The samplers in this book were all made with MEZ embroidery floss; the charts show the MEZ numbers. For those who prefer DMC or J. & P. Coats embroidery floss, the following numbers are suggested as possible alternatives.

MEZ	DMC	J. & P. COATS	MEZ	DMC	J. & P. COATS
01	Snow-white	1	359	300	238
02	ecru	61	360	433	81A
06	948	266	363	436	261
08	754	265	367	945	260
09	819	226	369	919	268
10	3326	46A	370	434	81
11	892	228	371	433	81A
19	817	229	373	435	62
22	304	229	374	434	81
26	603	59	375	436	51C
29	600	229	378	435	62
41	892	219	381	938	264
42	498	227	382	898	238
48	3689	65	387	712	61
49	776	65	390	739	266
50	963	226	397	762	70
59	815	143	398	415	71
68	326	120	399	415	71
75	3354	217	400	414	—
76	603	46	401	413	—
77	309	100	403	310	12
78	3350	143	778	963	226
95	211	65	832	433	262
98	550	36	843	3012	249
100	553	54	844	471	215
107	550	36	846	938	238
108	554	37	847	762	70
109	553	54	848	415	71
110	550	36	850	932	270
112	208	32	851	823	55
117	800	8	853	840	261
120	828	3	854	640	—
128	828	3	856	434	81
129	800	8	860	3346	249
130	809	69	862	367	109
131	799	245	868	554	37
132	796	44	869	211	—
133	824	44	870	554	37
146	825	76	871	3687	54
158	828	3	872	902	32
160	800	8	876	320	48
161	793	270	878	701	48A
164	824	44	880	745	9
167	3325	3	884	920	75A
185	747	201	892	353	265
188	993	222	893	776	65
300	744	43	896	918	241
302	725	255	897	3685	241
303	972	11	901	783	90A
304	741	38	903	780	51C
305	783	235	905	838	264
306	783	235	920	809	69
308	921	258	921	809	69
309	436	51C	922	311	108
316	920	75A	926	739	61
333	606	239	928	828	3
335	891	240	939	809	69
338	970	224	941	825	76
341	918	268	943	782	258
347	758	—	972	815	143
351	355	268	975	747	3
358	801	81B			

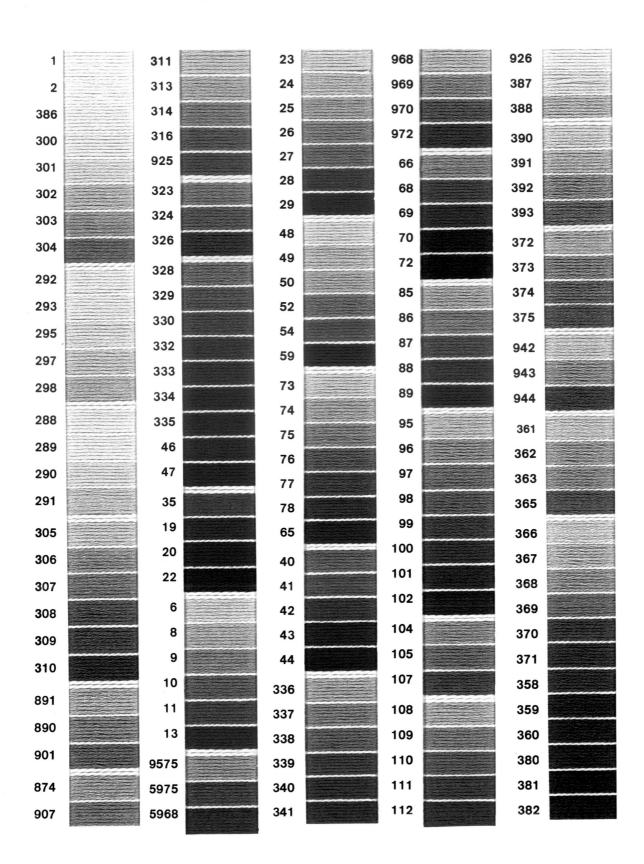

Color chart for MEZ ⚓ embroidery floss

When buying the embroidery floss, please note
the following: A zero in front of the color number
of the wrapper around the floss means that the
strand of floss is 8m (the normal length is 10).

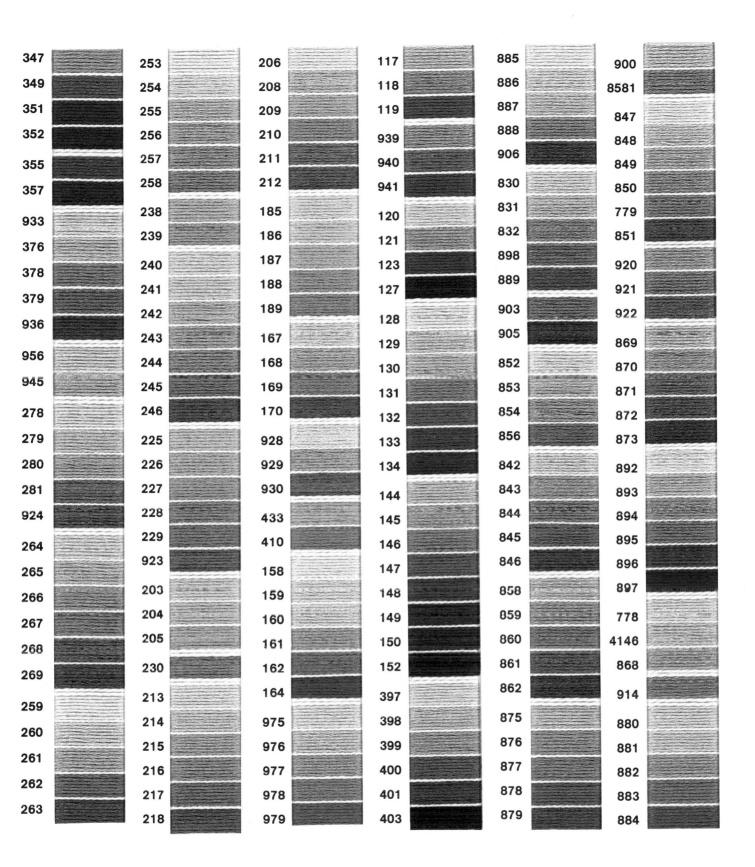

347
349
351
352
355
357
933
376
378
379
936
956
945
278
279
280
281
924
264
265
266
267
268
269
259
260
261
262
263

253
254
255
256
257
258
238
239
240
241
242
243
244
245
246
225
226
227
228
229
923
203
204
205
230
213
214
215
216
217
218

206
208
209
210
211
212
185
186
187
188
189
167
168
169
170
928
929
930
433
410
158
159
160
161
162
164
975
976
977
978
979

117
118
119
939
940
941
120
121
123
127
128
129
130
131
132
133
134
144
145
146
147
148
149
150
152
397
398
399
400
401
403

885
886
887
888
906
830
831
832
898
889
903
905
852
853
854
856
842
843
844
845
846
858
859
860
861
862
875
876
877
878
879

900
8581
847
848
849
850
779
851
920
921
922
869
870
871
872
873
892
893
894
895
896
897
778
4146
868
914
880
881
882
883
884

9

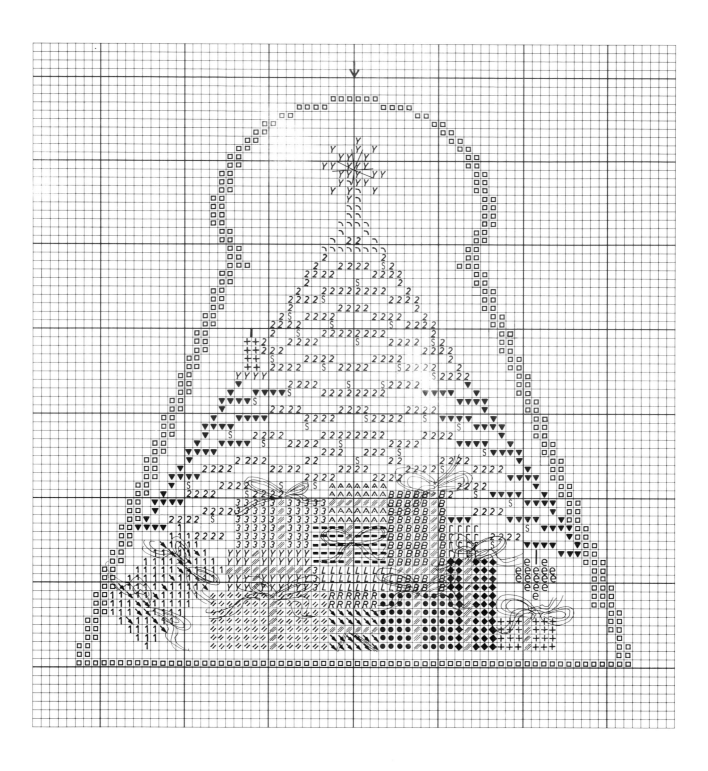

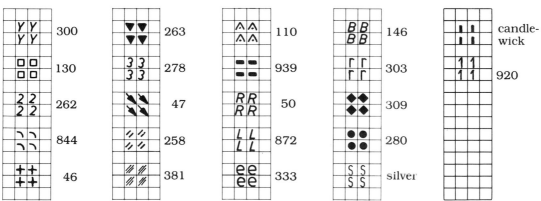

Y Y / Y Y	300	▼ ▼ / ▼ ▼	263
□ □ / □ □	130	3 3 / 3 3	278
2 2 / 2 2	262	◥ ◥	47
⌐ ⌐ / ⌐ ⌐	844	⁄⁄ ⁄⁄ / ⁄⁄ ⁄⁄	258
+ + / + +	46	∥ ∥ / ∥ ∥	381

∧ ∧ / ∧ ∧	110	B B / B B	146
▬ ▬ / ▬ ▬	939	Γ Γ / Γ Γ	303
R R / R R	50	◆ ◆ / ◆ ◆	309
L L / L L	872	● ● / ● ●	280
e e / e e	333	S S / S S	silver

I I / I I	candle-wick
1 1 / 1 1	920

This design includes Christmas gift boxes with pretty bows under the tree.

To create them, use three strands and make only half a cross-stitch—the understitch. The beginning and end of the thread is left long enough in order to tie the bow.

Area of finished embroidery: 5¼″ × 5½″ (13.3 × 13.8 cm).

ZZ / ZZ	305	◢◣ / ◢◣	112	DD / DD	226	77 / 77	943	33 / 33	278	MM / MM	26	⌇⌇ / ⌇⌇	403
GG / GG	158	◥◤ / ◢◣	49	■□ / □■	359	ꭆꭆ / ꭆꭆ	76	ᒥᒥ / ᒥᒥ	303	÷÷ / ÷÷	78	⌇⌇ / ⌇⌇	403
⌄⌄ / ⌄⌄	160	ii / ii	95	◆◆ / ◆◆	309	øø / øø	09	++ / ++	46	99 / 99	398	// / //	860
⌀⌀ / ⌀⌀	100	▬▬ / ▬▬	161	ꭇꭇ / ꭇꭇ	941	AA / AA	843	↘↘ / ↘↘	47	VV / VV	387		

This project is accomplished best by starting at the tablecloth and working from there upwards to the trunk of the Christmas tree and likewise upwards to do the rest of the tree. Next follow with the little girl and then the cat. Do the border last!

Area of finished embroidery: 5½″ × 7″ (14 × 17.5 cm).

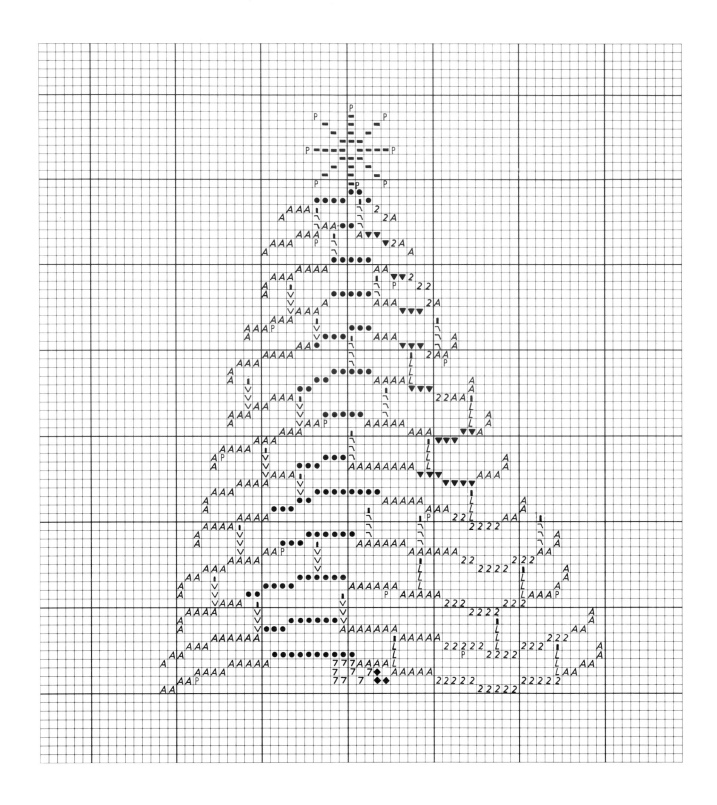

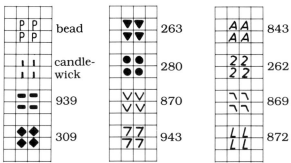

P P / P P — bead	▼▼ / ▼▼ — 263	A A / A A — 843
ı ı / ı ı — candle-wick	● ● / ● ● — 280	2 2 / 2 2 — 262
▬ ▬ / ▬ ▬ — 939	V V / V V — 870	╗ ╗ / ╗ ╗ — 869
◆ ◆ / ◆ ◆ — 309	7 7 / 7 7 — 943	L L / L L — 872

Although the canvas here has a different weave count, 1 cm of canvas still accommodates 4½ cross-stitches and there are two threads to a cross-stitch with a No. 22 needle.

In the pattern on the opposite page, you will find the letter *P*. That indicates the place to add a little glass bead (to simulate a Christmas decoration).

Area of finished embroidery: 4¾″ × 6″ (12 × 15 cm).

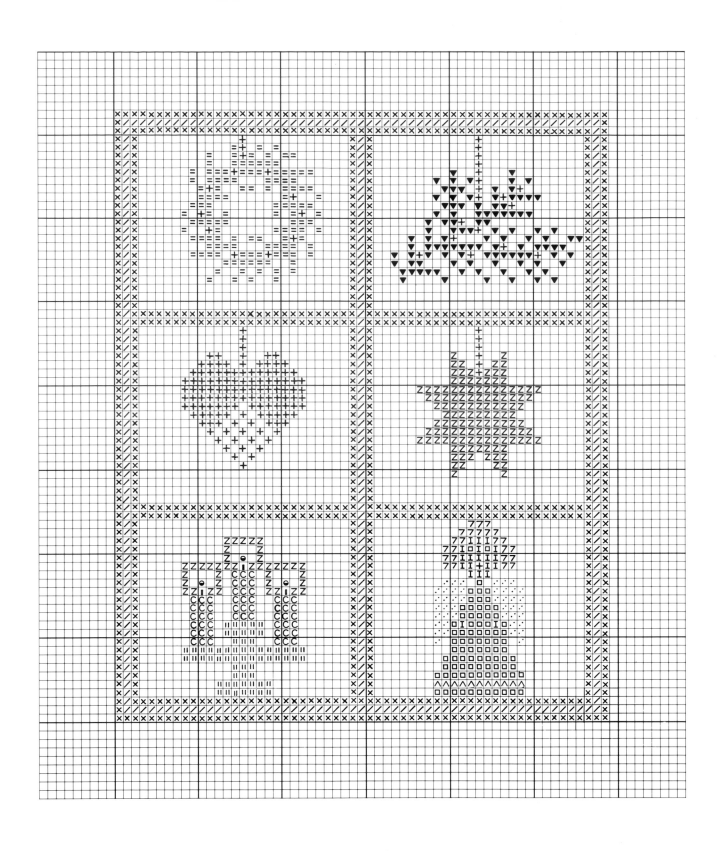

XX / XX	858	
// / //	860	
== / ==	246	

++ / ++	46	
▼▼ / ▼▼	263	
ZZ / ZZ	305	

‖‖ / ‖‖	903	
CC / CC	306	
ςς / ςς	403	

·.· / ·.·	847	
77 / 77	943	
II / II	06	

▫▫ / ▫▫	130	
∧∧ / ∧∧	292	

This design can also be used for Christmas cards when each individual section is used by itself.

Area of finished embroidery: 4¼″ × 5½″ (11 × 14 cm).

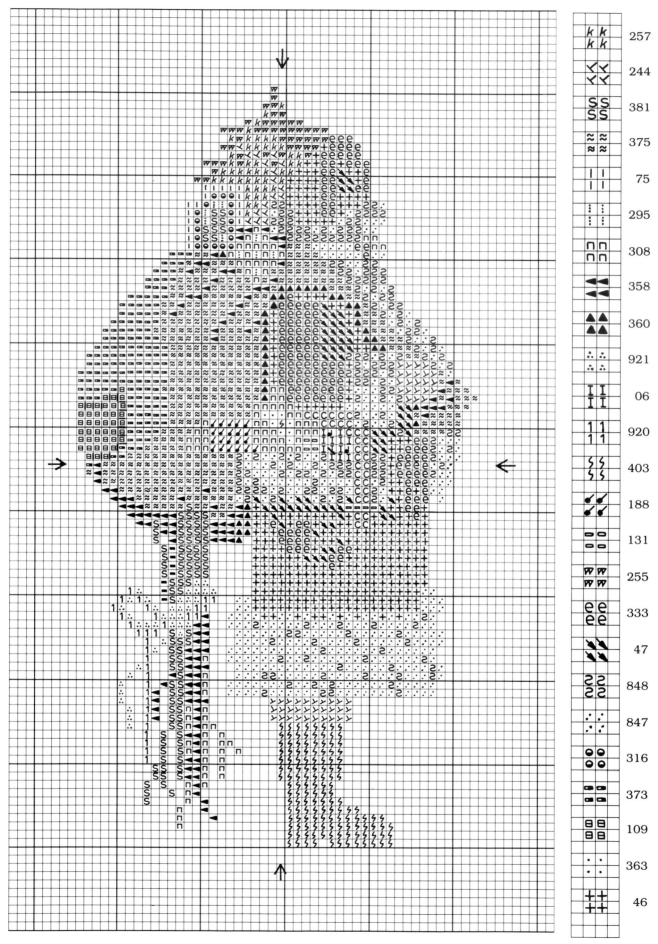

k k / k k	257
≺ / ≺	244
S S / S S	381
≈ ≈ / ≈ ≈	375
I I / I I	75
⋮ ⋮ / ⋮ ⋮	295
⊓ ⊓ / ⊓ ⊓	308
◄ ◄ / ◄ ◄	358
▲ ▲ / ▲ ▲	360
∴ ∴ / ∴ ∴	921
I I / I I	06
1 1 / 1 1	920
ϟ ϟ / ϟ ϟ	403
✔ ✔ / ✔ ✔	188
▭ ▭ / ▭ ▭	131
W W / W W	255
e e / e e	333
�’ �’ / ➘ ➘	47
ℶ ℶ / ℶ ℶ	848
∴ ∴ / ∴ ∴	847
◉ ◉ / ◉ ◉	316
▬ ▬ / ▬ ▬	373
8 8 / 8 8	109
∴ ∴ / ∴ ∴	363
+ + / + +	46

18

C C C C	306
Y Y Y Y	281

This Santa Claus is complete with toys and gingerbread. This design requires much concentration since the shading of the colors is very subtle (*design by Katja M. Hassler*).

Area of finished embroidery: 3¾″ × 6¾″ (9.5 × 17 cm).

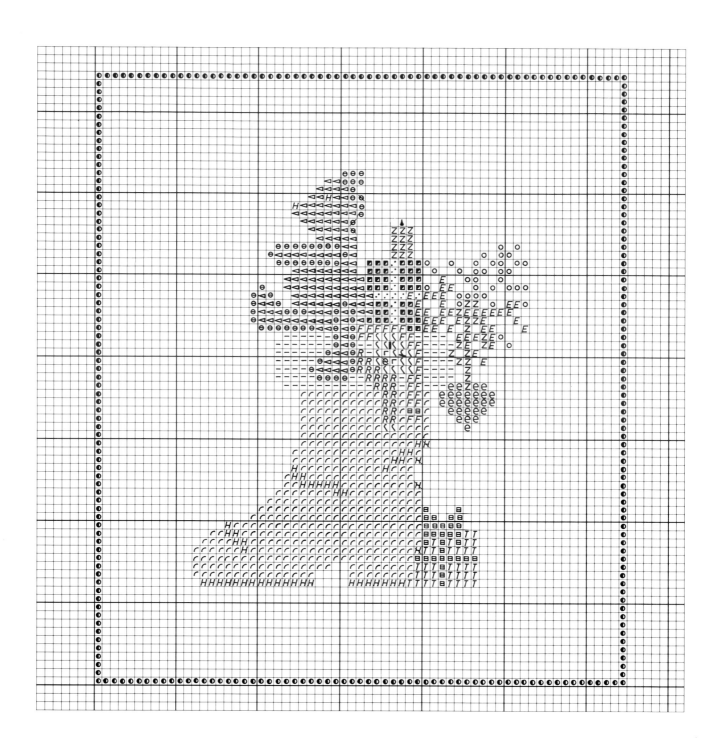

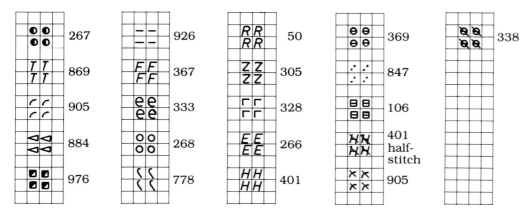

267	926	50
869	367	305
905	333	328
884	268	266
976	778	401

369	338
847	
106	
401 half-stitch	
905	

This Santa Claus boot is stuffed with toys and goodies. The design can be reduced by moving the border closer to the picture or by eliminating it altogether.

Area of finished embroidery: 4¾″ × 5½″ (12 × 14 cm).

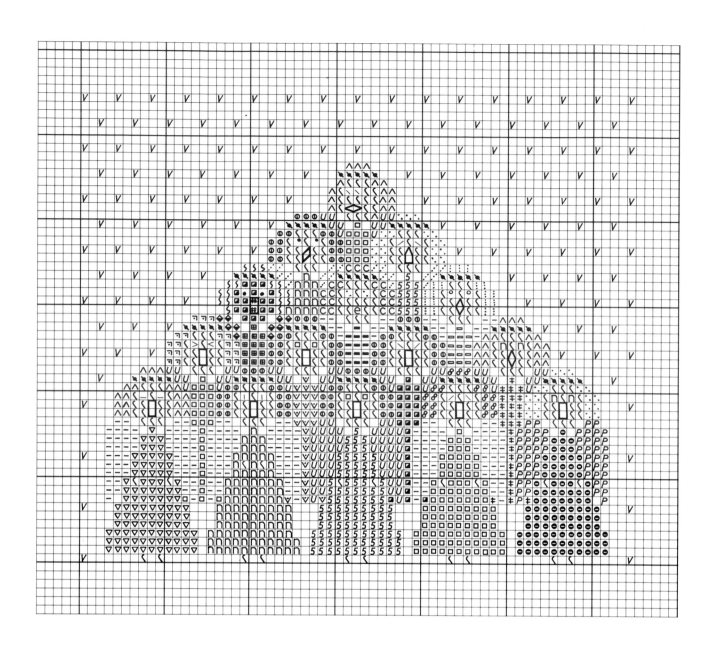

V V / V V	387	
▬ ▭ / ▬ ▭	131	
◼ ◼ / ◼ ◼	359	
∧ ∧ / ∧ ∧	292	
◐ ◐ / ◐ ◐	185	
— — / — —	926	
⌐ ⌐ / ⌐ ⌐	347	

∴∵ / ∴∵	02	
Φ Φ / Φ Φ	891	
▽ ▽ / ▽ ▽	928	
⊞ ⊞ / ⊞ ⊞	48	
⧣ ⧣ / ⧣ ⧣	306	
⋒ ⋒ / ⋒ ⋒	120	
◥ ◥ / ◥ ◥	silver	

5 5 / 5 5	128	
P P / P P	390	
◆ ◆ / ◆ ◆	399	
U U / U U	397	
▢ ▢ / ▢ ▢	130	
⟨ ⟨ / ⟨ ⟨	778	
∴∵ / ∴∵	378	

‡ ‡ / ‡ ‡	129	
ⱽ ⱽ / ⱽ ⱽ	167	
⋮ ⋮ / ⋮ ⋮	295	
▬ ▬ / ▬ ▬	939	
⟩ ⟩ / ⟩ ⟩	403	

The little brown angel in pink underscores the tender and heavenly atmosphere created by this choir of angels in blue robes. Of course you can change some or all of the color—either the color of the hair and/or the robes.

Area of finished embroidery: 4″ × 4¾″ (10.3 × 12.3 cm).

~ ~ / ~ ~	302	
·.· / ·.·	847	
6 6 / 6 6	341	
◆◆ / ◆◆	309	
6 6 / 6 6	370	

▲▲ / ▲▲	360	
·:· / ·:·	400	
9 9 / 9 9	398	
~ ~ / ~ ~	371	
1 1 / 1 1	920	

·.· / ·.·	921	
I I / I I	06	
C C / C C	306	
/ / / /	860	
P P / P P	390	

X X / X X	858	
►► / ►►	896	
0 0 / 0 0	854	
⌃⌃ / ⌃⌃	892	
◇◇ / ◇◇	897	

⊙⊙ / ⊙⊙	369	
a a / a a	922	
✶✶ / ✶✶	382	
◩◩ / ◩◩	359	
⌐⌐ / ⌐⌐	846	

The choice of earth-tone colors for the nativity scene is an attempt to underscore the simplicity of the scene.

Area of finished embroidery: 5⅛″ × 5¼″ (13 × 13.5 cm).

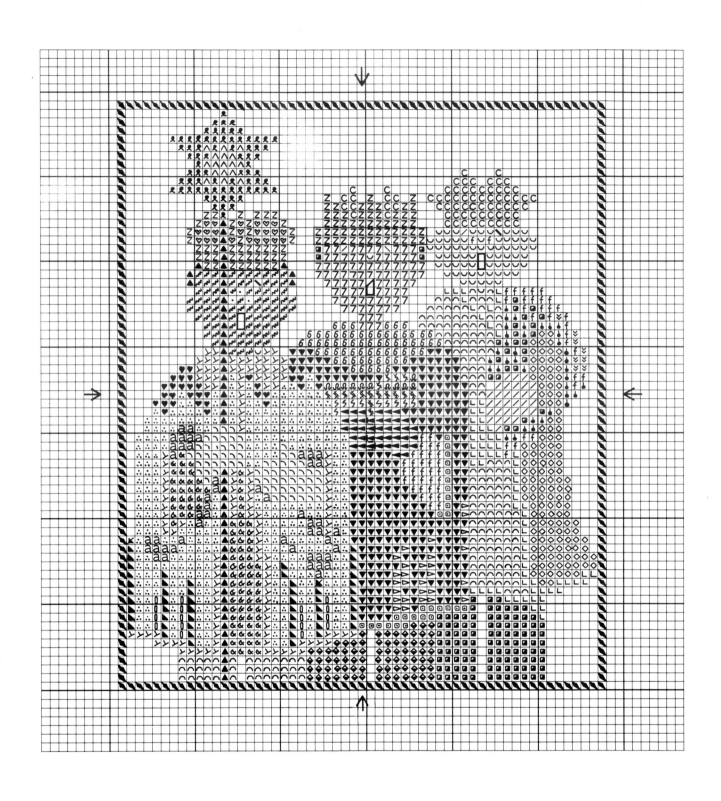

♟♟♟♟	291	ΩΩΩΩ	01	∩∩∩∩	972	⩔⩔⩔⩔	874	⟨⟨⟨⟨	403	◀◀◀◀	358	∪∪∪∪	302
CCCC	306	♥♥♥♥	850	▷▷▷▷	878	ZZZZ	305	∴∴∴∴	363	▫▫▫▫	359	6666	341
♦♦♦♦	374	&&&&	851	∴∴∴∴	921	7777	943	////	860	▼▼▼▼	263	▫▫▫▫	19
♣♣♣♣	880	♡♡♡♡	68	⌐⌐⌐⌐	844	◩◩◩◩	204	ffff	901	⟨⟨⟨⟨	403 half-stitch	▲▲▲▲	162
∧∧∧∧	292	YYYY	281	◇◇◇◇	399	LLLL	871	0000	164	▲▲▲▲	360	◇◇◇◇	847

26

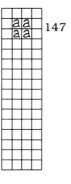 147

The eyes of these small carolers are made by using only understitches—pointing sideways towards each other. The lips are straight stitches covering two blocks in the vertical direction and one in the horizontal direction. Use vertical straight stitches for the line-marking of the pages in the song book.

Area of finished embroidery: 4¼″ × 5″ (10.7 × 12.7 cm).

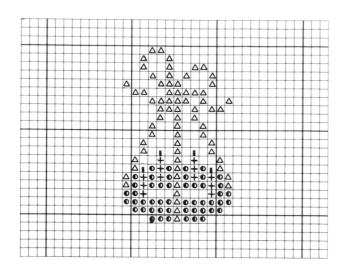

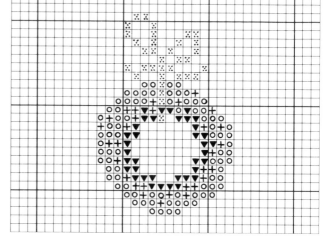

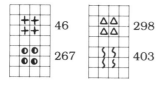

+ + / + +	46		△ △ / △ △	298	
◐ ◐ / ◐ ◐	267		∫ ∫ / ∫ ∫	403	

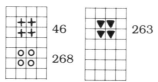

+ + / + +	46		▼ ▼ / ▼ ▼	263	
◐ ◐ / ◐ ◐	268				

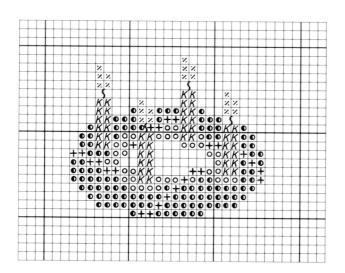

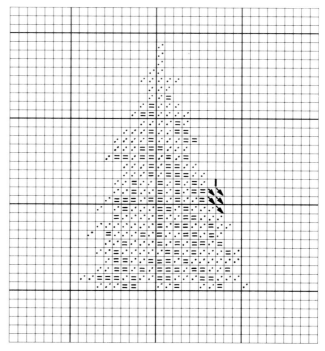

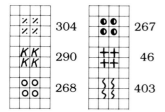

⅍ ⅍ / ⅍ ⅍	304		◐ ◐ / ◐ ◐	267	
K K / K K	290		+ + / + +	46	
◐ ◐ / ◐ ◐	268		∫ ∫ / ∫ ∫	403	

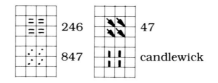

= = / = =	246		◥◣ / ◥◣	47	
⋰ ⋱ / ⋱ ⋰	847		I I / I I	candlewick	

The sizes: Wreath with yellow bow 1″ × 1½″
(2.5 × 4 cm).

Wreath with red bow 1½″ × 1¾″
(3.8 × 4.5 cm).

Wreath with candles 1½″ × 1¾″
(3.8 × 4.5 cm).

Christmas tree with snow 1½″ ×
2½″ (4 × 6.2 cm).

These are four small designs specifically suitable for Christmas cards. They are very easy to make and look very beautiful when framed in paper mounts (*passe-partout*). The mounts can be obtained readymade as well as being very easy to make.

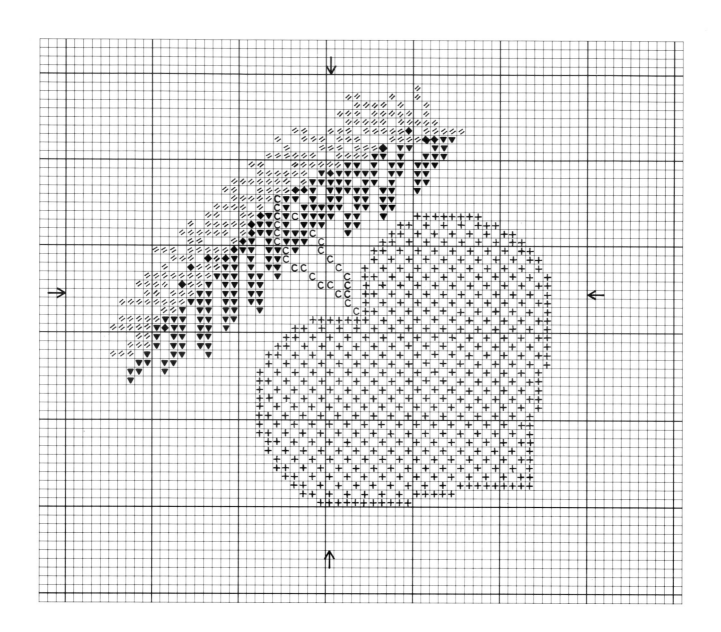

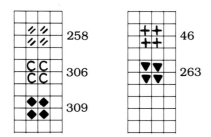

🔳 258	➕ 46
C 306	▼ 263
◆ 309	

The diagonal position of the heart motif gives this design its unusual flavor. The arrows mark the vertical and horizontal midline, which ought to make the counting a little easier.

Area of finished embroidery: 4″ × 4″ (10 × 10 cm).

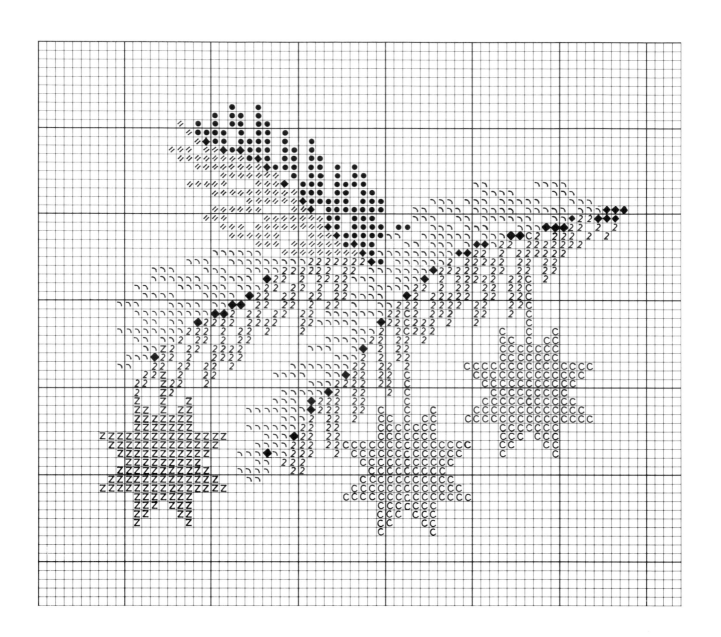

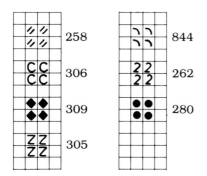

	258
	844
	306
	262
	309
	280
	305

This design—a branch with stars—is especially suitable for an ornament. A star taken by itself could also be used as a Christmas card motif.

Area of finished embroidery: 3¾" × 4½" (9.7 × 11.5 cm).

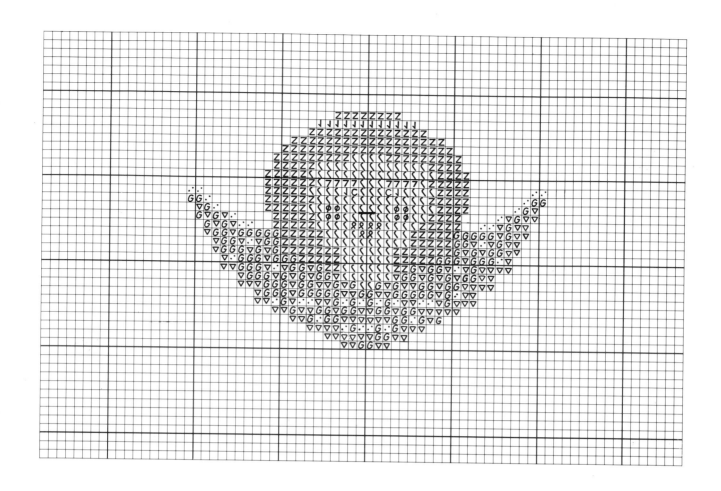

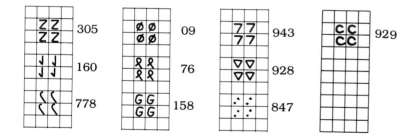

ZZ / ZZ	305
↵↵ / ↵↵	160
⟨⟨ / ⟨⟨	778

øø / øø	09
႙႙ / ႙႙	76
GG / GG	158

77 / 77	943
▽▽ / ▽▽	928
·.·. / ·.·.	847

CC / CC	929

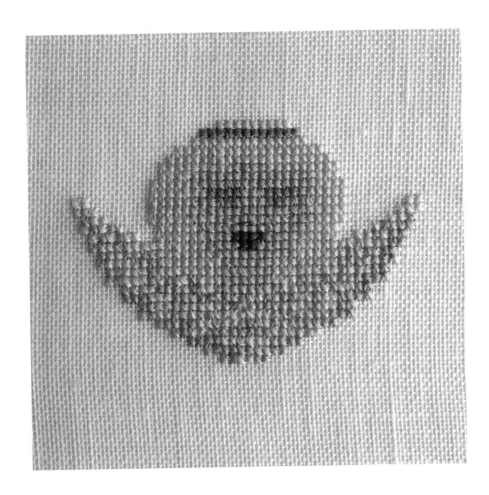

The little angel can be done in no time at all and is as useful for decorating a napkin, a place mat or a little handbag, as it is for a Christmas card.

Area of finished embroidery: 2¼" × 3¼" (5.9 × 8.5 cm).

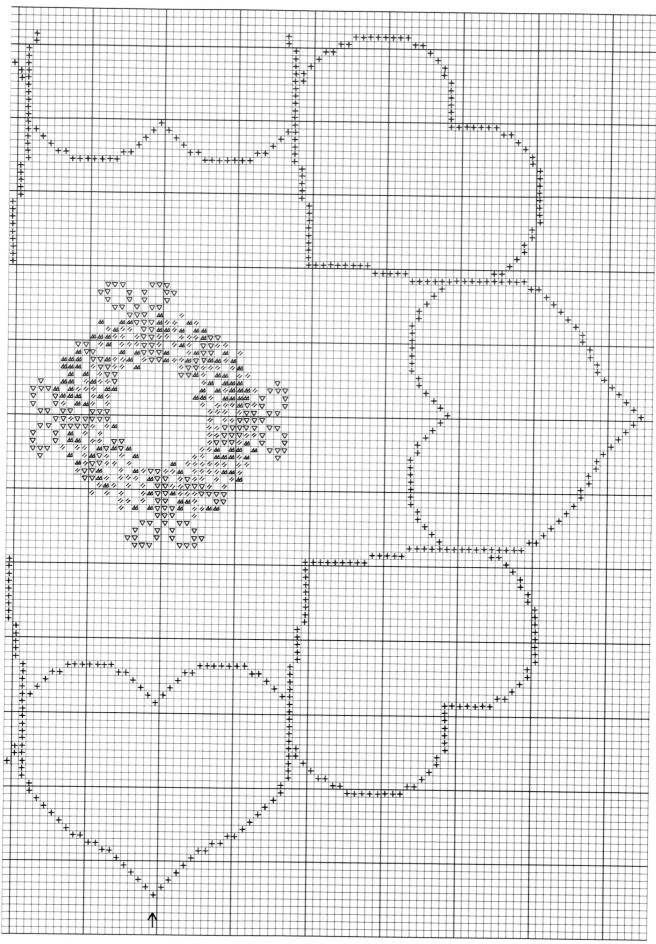

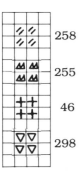

// // // //	258
⋏⋏ ⋏⋏ ⋏⋏ ⋏⋏	255
┼┼ ┼┼	46
▽▽ ▽▽	298

This is a perfect design for a Christmas table-cloth or cover with the use of traditional colors. A more lively design can be created by either filling in every other heart partially, as shown on page 45, or fully.

Area of finished embroidery from point to point in both directions: 10″ (25.5 cm).

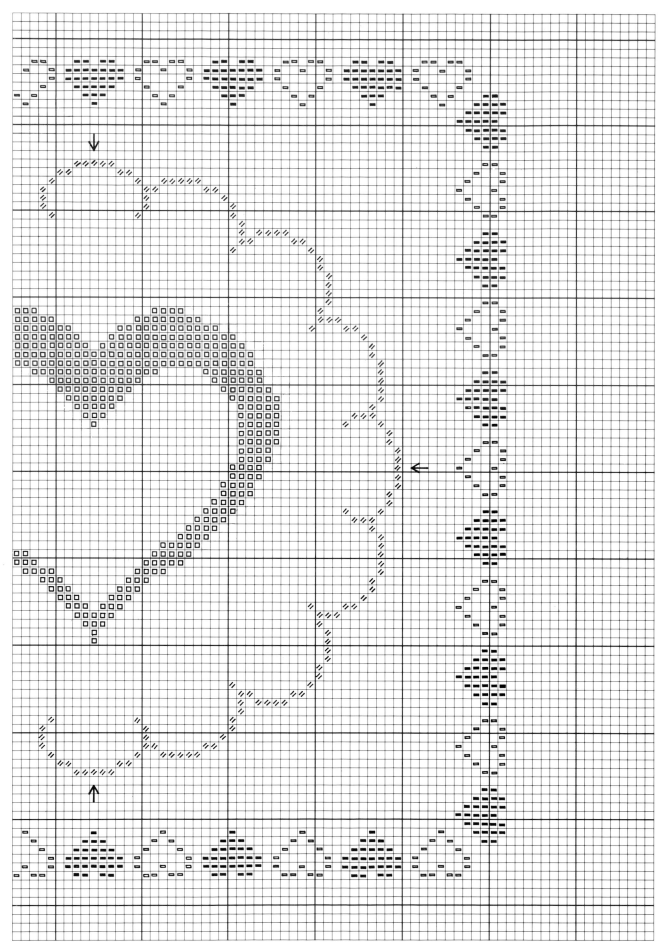

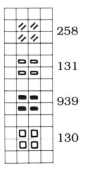

	258
	131
	939
	130

This square design is perfect for a pillow or a tablecloth. The colors do not limit its use or display to the Christmas season. The border is excellent for napkins and place mats.

Area of finished embroidery: 7½″ × 7¾″ (19 × 19.5 cm).

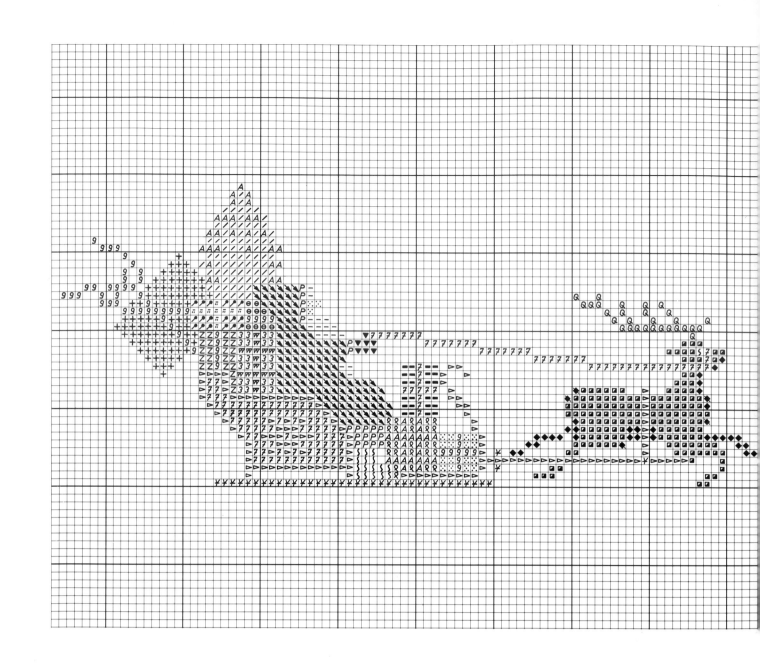

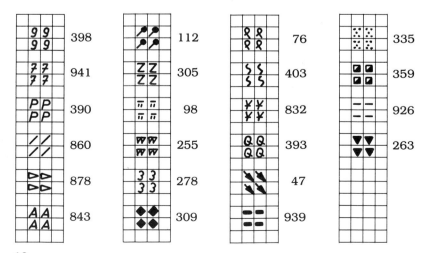

9 9 / 9 9	398	
7 7 / 7 7	941	
P P / P P	390	
/ / / / /	860	
▷▷ / ▷▷	878	
A A / A A	843	

♪♪ / ♪♪	112	
Z Z / Z Z	305	
ᵖᵖ / ᵖᵖ	98	
₩₩ / ₩₩	255	
3 3 / 3 3	278	
◆◆ / ◆◆	309	

R R / R R	76	
ς ς / ς ς	403	
¥ ¥ / ¥ ¥	832	
Q Q / Q Q	393	
◥◥ / ◥◥	47	
▬▬ / ▬▬	939	

⋰⋰ / ⋰⋰	335	
◪◪ / ◪◪	359	
– – / – –	926	
▼▼ / ▼▼	263	

This is Santa Claus in a real hurry. The design
is particularly suitable for a table runner. It is
easy to add to the length of the motif (when a
longer piece of material is used) by lengthening
Santa's reins and the shaft of the sled. Of course
reindeers can also be added (*design by Katja M.
Hassler*).

Area of finished embroidery: 3″ × 6¾″ (7.5 ×
17 cm).

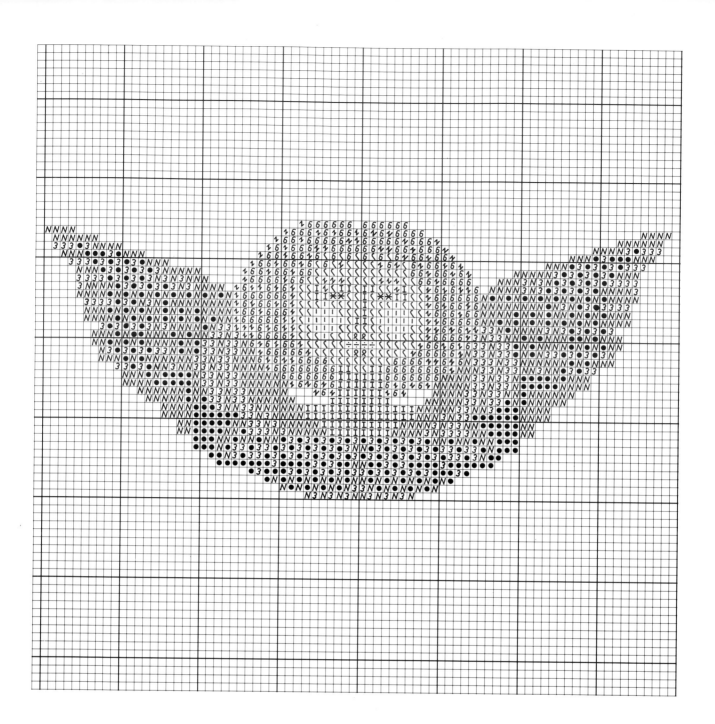

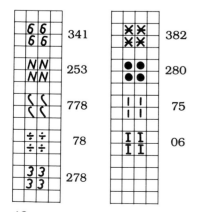

6 6 / 6 6	341	
N N / N N	253	
⟨ ⟨ / ⟨ ⟨	778	
÷ ÷ / ÷ ÷	78	
3 3 / 3 3	278	

✕ ✕ / ✕ ✕	382	
● ● / ● ●	280	
∣ ∣ / ∣ ∣	75	
I I / I I	06	

This angel is not quite as sweet as most Christmas angels are with those unusual wings and the reddish hair. But that makes it suitable as a guardian angel, or as an ornament on a christening gown (use stramin when embroidering), or as a housewarming gift, either in the form of a greeting card or framed for a picture (*design by Katja M. Hassler*).

Area of finished embroidery: 3″ × 6″ (7.5 × 15 cm).

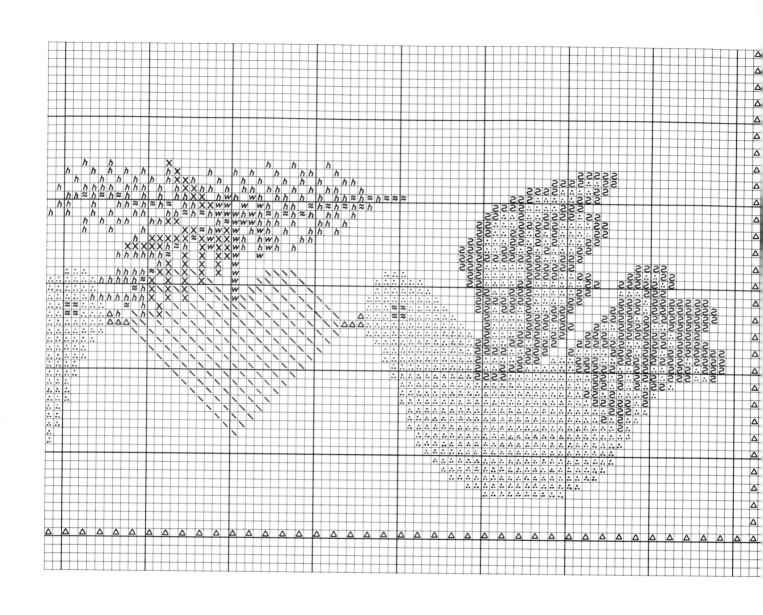

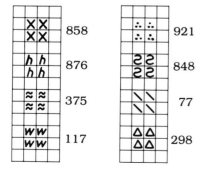

X X / X X	858	
h h / h h	876	
≈ ≈ / ≈ ≈	375	
w w / w w	117	

∴ ∴ / ∴ ∴	921	
౭ ౭ / ౭ ౭	848	
\ \ / \ \	77	
△ △ / △ △	298	

This adaptable design, too, can be used on many different projects such as table runners, place mats or napkins. The motifs can all be used in different combinations or individually.

Area of finished embroidery without the border: 3″ × 8½″ (7.5 × 21.3 cm).

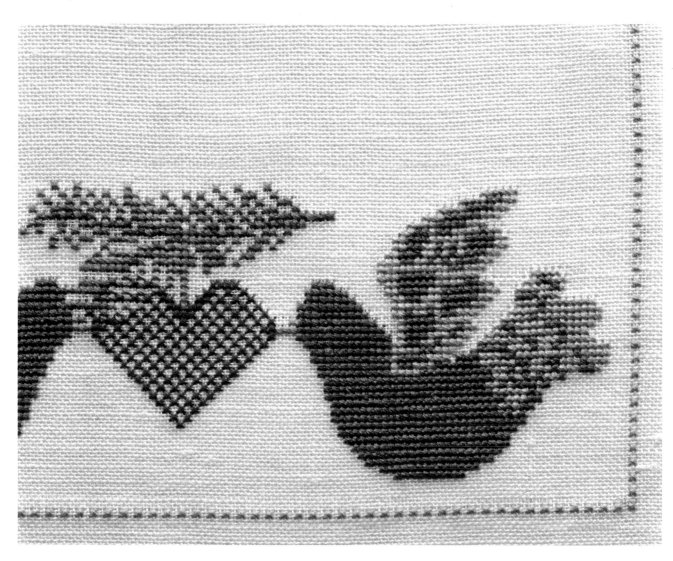

45

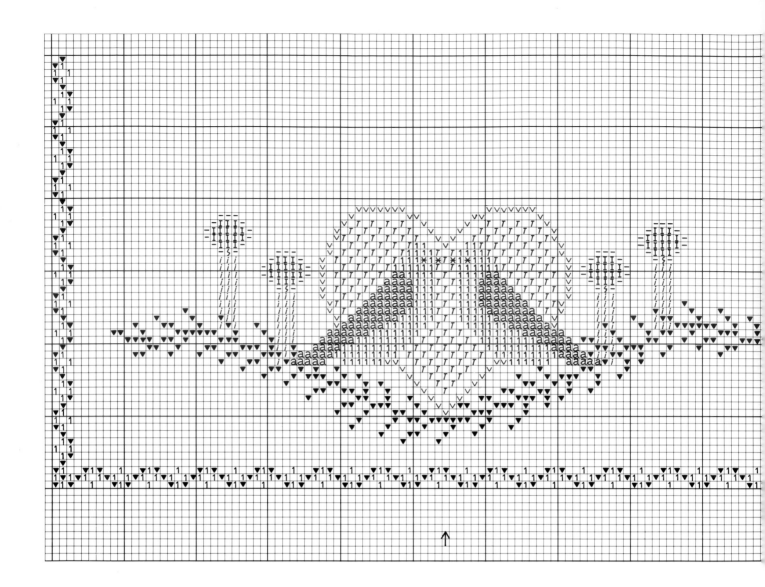

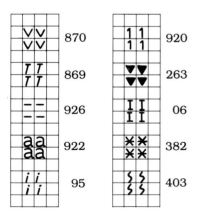

⌵⌵ / ⌵⌵	870	1 1 / 1 1	920
I I / I I	869	▼▼ / ▼▼	263
− − / − −	926	I I / I I	06
a a / a a	922	✕✕ / ✕✕	382
i i / i i	95	⟩⟩ / ⟩⟩	403

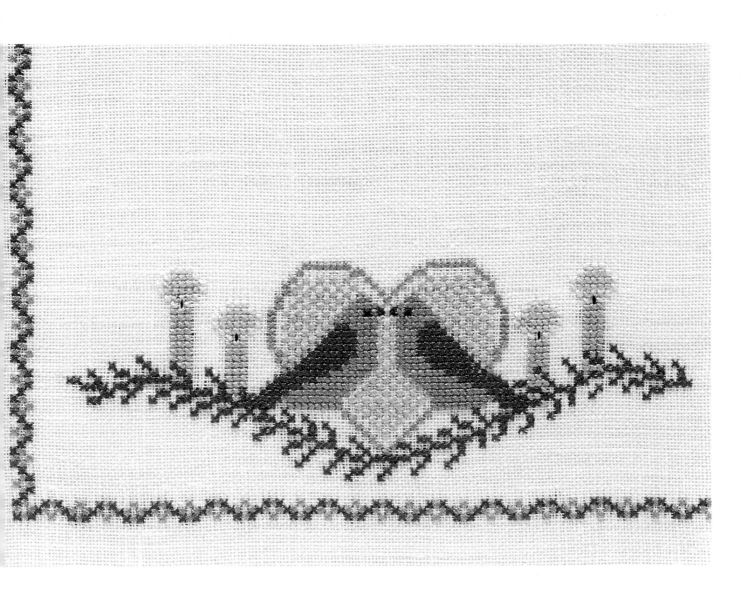

This design is ideal for a table runner and several variations are possible: one could use the birds alone, or use the heart alone (filling in the appropriate space left without the birds). The border of course is carried around the whole piece.

Area of finished embroidery without the border: 2¾″ × 7″ (7 × 17.5 cm).

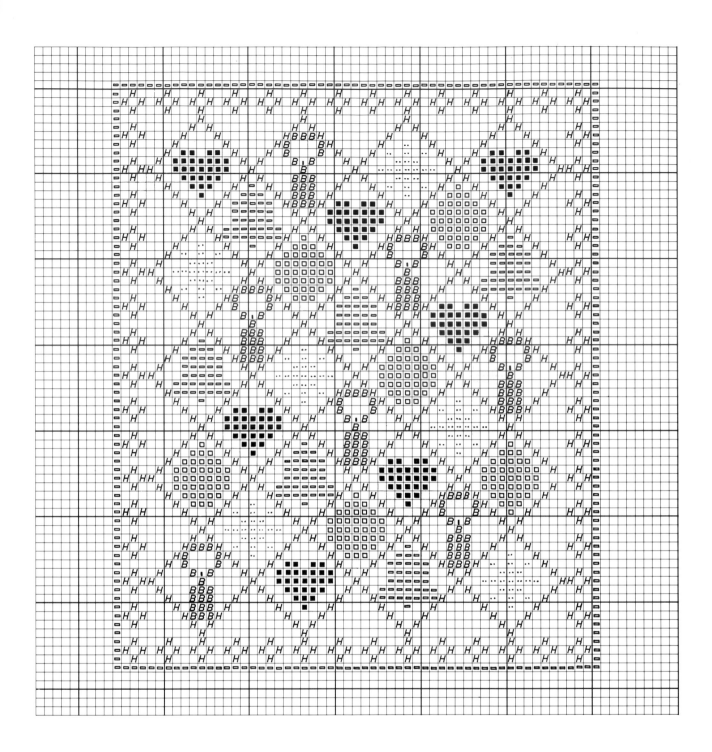

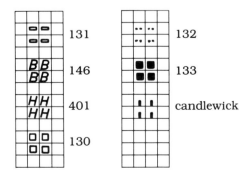

131

132

146

133

401

candlewick

130

48

This design would be excellent as decoration for a folder that holds Christmas cards, as the cover for a book, scrapbook, or album.

Area of finished embroidery: 4⅛″ × 5⅛″ (10.5 × 13 cm).

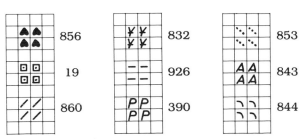 856	¥¥ / ¥¥ 832	∴∴ / ∴∴ 853
19	– – / – – 926	AA / AA 843
/ / / / 860	PP / PP 390	⌐⌐ / ⌐⌐ 844

The mistletoe, a symbol of forgiveness, has long made its way across the ocean to Germany. It is displayed above the door at Christmas time and it sccmcd appropriate to capture this sign of peace in a more durable form (*design by Katja M. Hassler*).

Area of finished embroidery: 4¾" × 7" (12 × 17.6 cm).

Here are Christmas trees in all shapes and sizes to choose from. This is a sampler in its truest form. If chosen as a border motif, or a tree by itself or a row of them, one is assured of finding the right one. And as a bonus: hearts and stars! On pages 56–57 the sampler has been duplicated, doubled in size.

Area of the finished embroidery, including border: 7¾″ × 11¾″ (19.5 × 30 cm).

Symbol	Color
~ ~ / ~ ~	302
/ / / /	860
1 1 / 1 1	920
Ş Ş / Ş Ş	silver
< < / < <	42
2 2 / 2 2	262
ℜ ℜ / ℜ ℜ	76
⅂ ⅂ / ⅂ ⅂	846
⊔ ⊔ / ⊔ ⊔	977
⊙ ⊙ / ⊙ ⊙	859
e e / e e	333
▫ ▫ / ▫ ▫	976
▷ ▷ / ▷ ▷	878
A A / A A	843
⊙ ⊙ / ⊙ ⊙	316
Z Z / Z Z	305

Symbol	Color
\ \ / \ \	77
I I / I I	75
+ + / + +	46
S S / S S	silver
¥ ¥ / ¥ ¥	832
L L / L L	872
▬ ▬ / ▬ ▬	939
B B / B B	146
⅃ ⅃ / ⅃ ⅃	216
∴ ∴ / ∴ ∴	269
‡ ‡ / ‡ ‡	263
◉ ◉ / ◉ ◉	267
7 7 / 7 7	941
∧ ∧ / ∧ ∧	110
I I / I I	candlewick
⋀	267

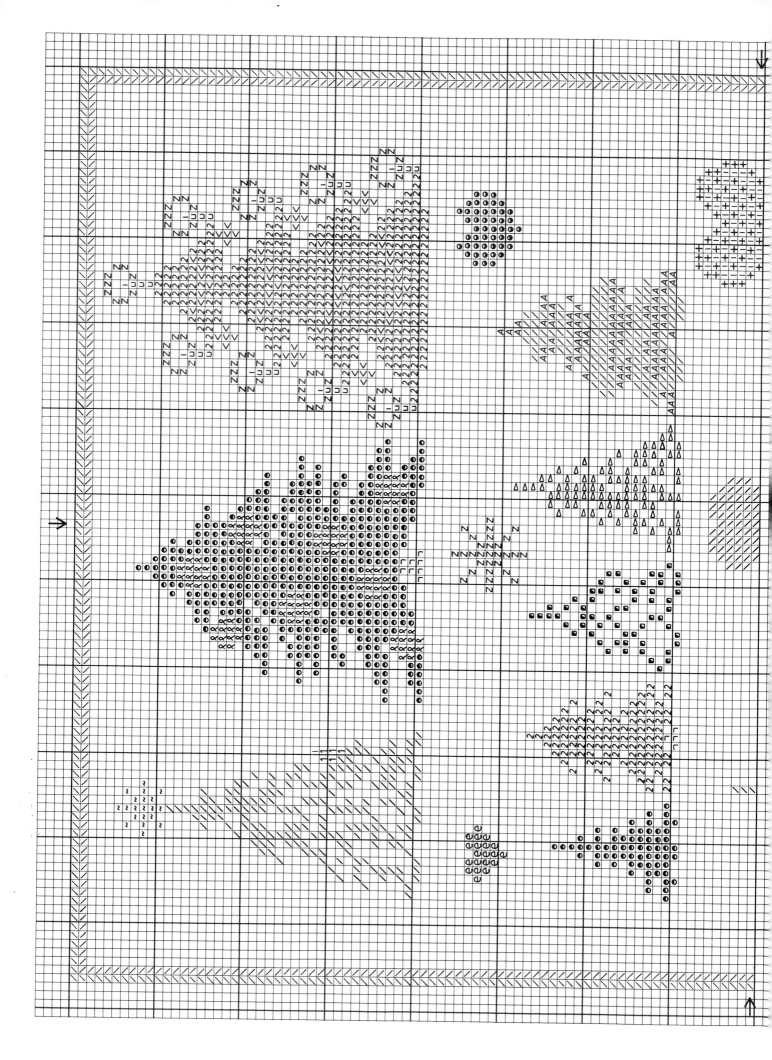

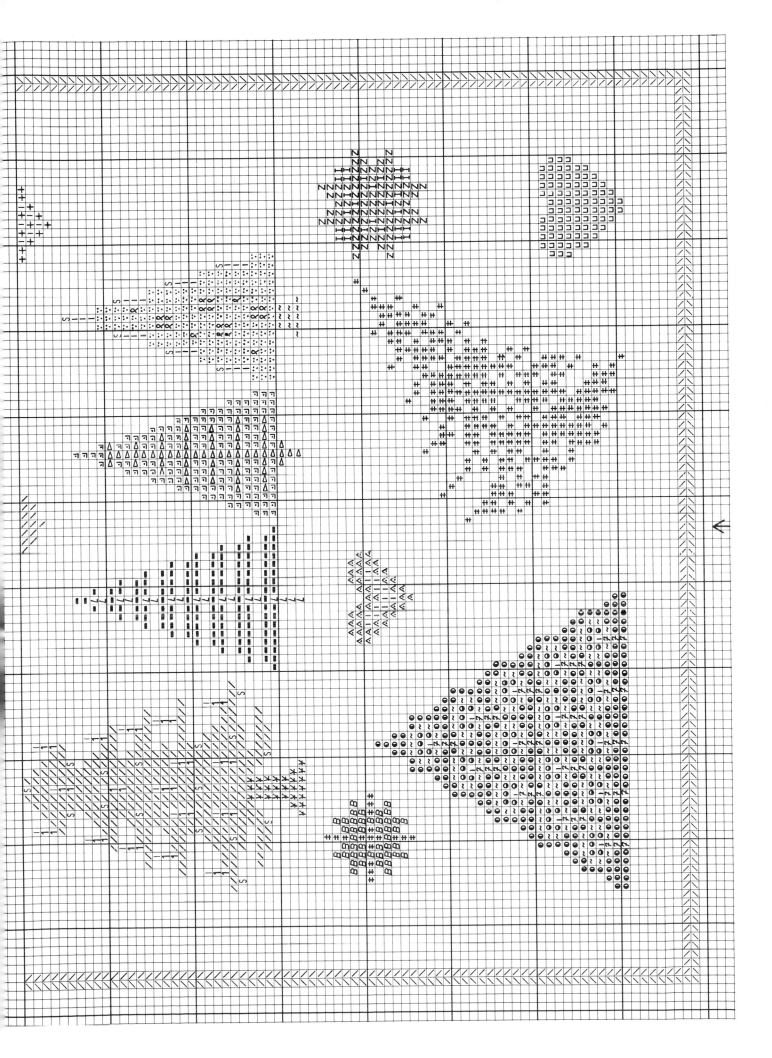

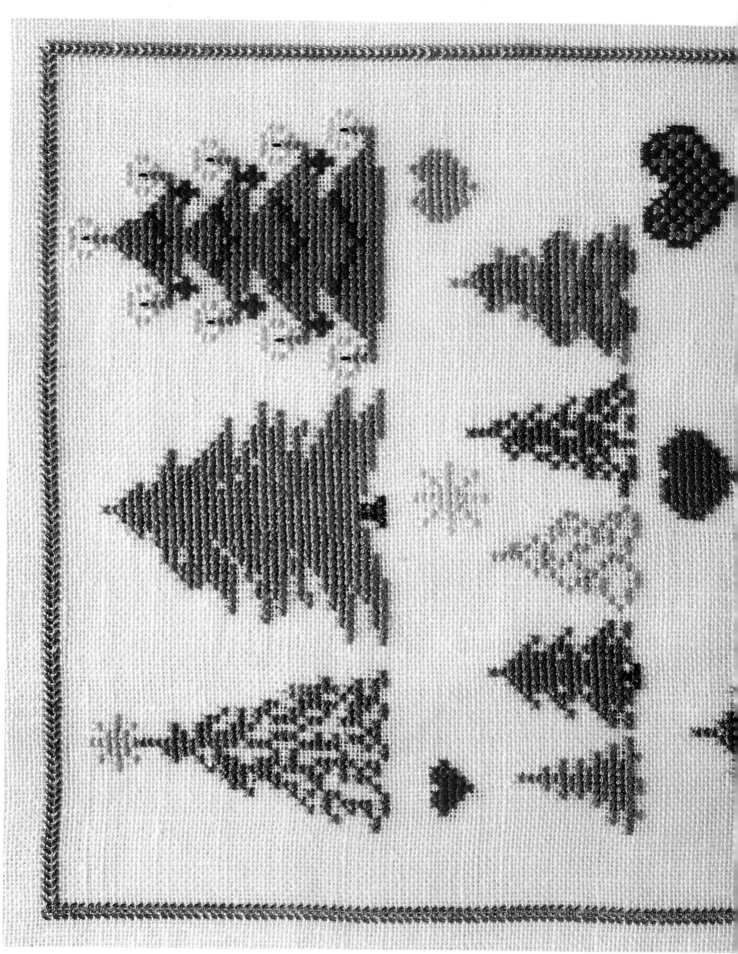

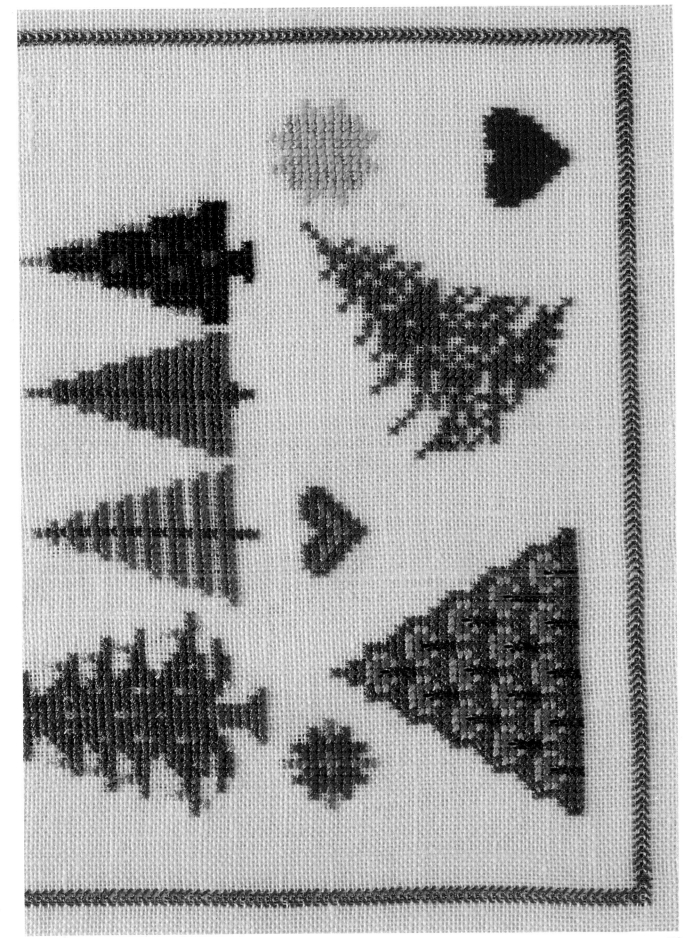

This beautiful sampler requires a considerable amount of time (approximately 30 hours) as well as a considerable amount of concentration. If you want to be able to finish it by Christmas, it is best to start this project early.

Start with the row of letters on the bottom, left or right to the center and work to the outside. Follow with the row of letters immediately above. Next continue with the row of letters on both sides (the vertical row), followed by the two rows on top and after that the candles and the inner border.

Once that is done it should be fairly easy to count out the stitches for the designs in the inner portion of the sampler. The angels and their wings on the top and bottom should be next followed by the green tree twigs on both sides. Conclude the project with the very outer border. The choice of color is only a suggestion. One does not need to search high and low for a color that is needed only for a very small design. Make use of what you already have at hand.

In case the sampler is to be framed, enough material must extend beyond its outer border so that the canvas can easily be mounted on a cardboard. Furthermore, since the sampler requires a considerable amount of canvas, it is best to overcast the outer edges of the material to prevent unnecessary fraying.

The different motifs within the sampler can all be used in different combination for a variety of projects: They all can be used by themselves for greeting cards or included in various combinations such as table runners, napkins and place mats and many more. Let your imagination soar. On pages 60–61 you will find the sampler again. The pattern is on pages 62–63.

Color		Color		Color
862	130	75
926	369	108
371	246	398
976	898	850
47	217	258
46	263	335
59	375	41
856	216	832
359	29	262
922	302	847
975	941	76
131	860	109
22	858	851
19	338	95
278	candle-wick	48
06	921	
939	872	
360	303	
267	920	
290	48	
943	306	
298	893	
08	10	
11	half-stitch 860	
328	half-stitch 860	

60

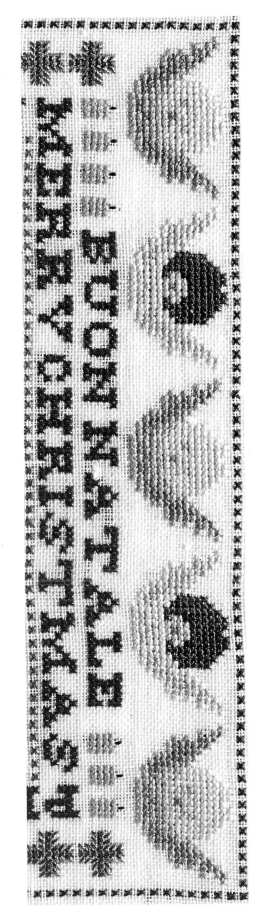

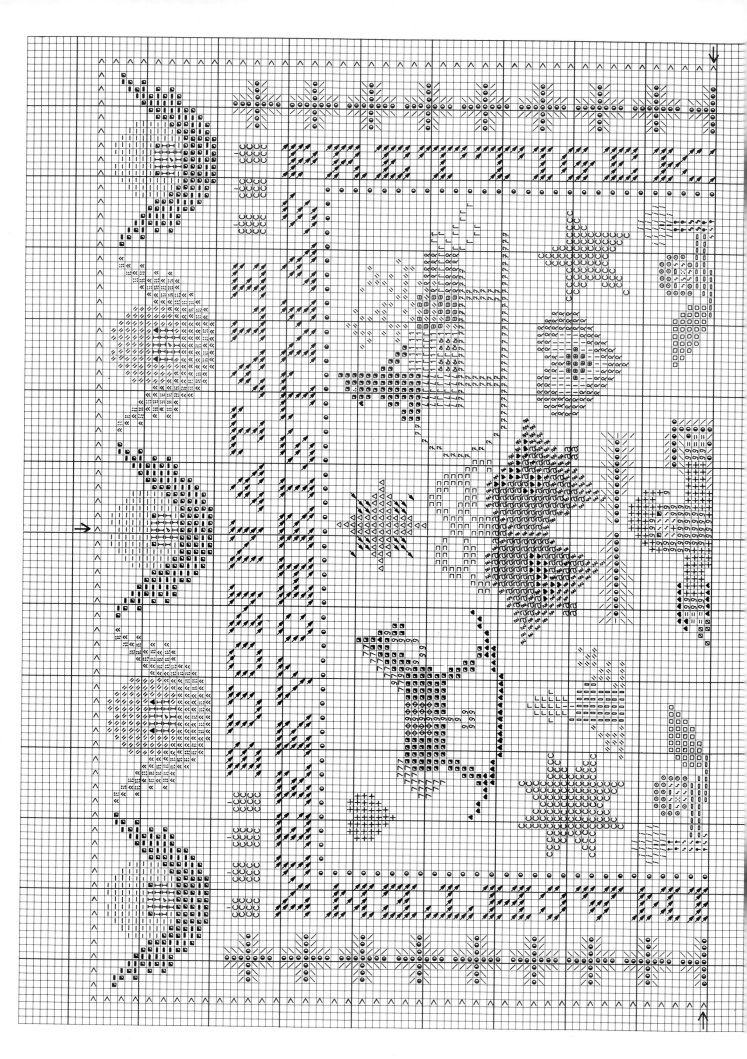

INDEX